Putting the Dog to Sleep

Damon Robinson

Presentation by *BookLeaf Publishing*

Web: www.bookleafpub.com

E-mail: info@bookleafpub.com

ISBN: 9789357615655

First edition 2022

This chapbook is dedicated to all of the people I have grown up with and how they have shaped me into who I am. I remember you, and the times we spoke. If you read this, lets speak again.

Cheers!

PREFACE

This book is a compilation of poems that have represented my experience adapting to adulthood. I believe that the day we grow up is the day we lose a big part of ourselves. The poetry in this book is a reflection of that journey and I hope you get something out of this. Topics such as loss, love, loneliness and more are talked about thoroughly within these pages. I have curated these poems from 2017 to now to properly catalogue the personal growth I've gone through in this time. A lot has happened, and I am sure we have all changed a lot in that time. It's a crazy world after all.

Childhood

They say childhood is the story of innocence lost. The time where the uninitiated learn what life is and its cost. It's when it's all said and done that we wish we could write a letter to our younger selves telling us everything we needed to say and what comes after.

But that's the funny part about childhood, you live many lives. To live like a nomad, wandering and wondering about the world and your place in the wildlands. To survive after heartbreak and heal and hear, hoping and unknowingly galloping headfirst into the next.

What is childhood if not a collection of stories and tall tales to tell those who will barely believe it. When we were kids we spun spools of fabrications into the daily news reports of our lives. Life was a fantasy back then, or at least we would hope it to be.

While some battled fantastical dragons in their bedrooms, others battled poverty and unpaid hydro bills. While some hid their report cards under the bed to avoid the wrath of their father, others hid from ghouls in their fortified pillow fort in the garage.

In many cases, childhood is a battleground that we carry war stories from. They can tell you all about how much they persevered. From how they felt after the great snowball war that decimated the snowman economy all the way to how they felt putting their dog to sleep.

All kids have lived many lives, and all kids have stories to tell. We always ask them what they want to be when they grow up. Little do they know, for most, all we will want to do is go back. Little do they know, the ones who win childhood are the ones who never fully grow up.

Cantaloupes

Why is there a cantaloupe,
in front of my orange juice
in the fridge?

For a month straight
I have to move it if I want orange
juice.

Who the frick
buys cantaloupes.

Soufris

You know that feeling,
where you talk to someone
and there are a few lines
of dialogue that happen to stand out
and you look at them a little differently.

I swear that I didn't notice
the light radiating around you before.
There was a buildup of sudden excitement
for something I wasn't looking for.
Maybe - but.. no - but maybe

I'm left to guess
what is happening,
having to to assume
that whatever this is
is both alive and dead
at the same time.

Things I Want to Say to You But Can't Because That Would Be Bit Weird

I wish you wore your hair down more,
because I am convinced that you tie yourself up
too much
over the things you cannot control, let it flow.

I tried to go slow, but the fact of the matter is
I only had the courage to stop by your window
just so I can hear what your voice sounded like.

I had no plan, there was no scheme
It's just that for the first time it seemed
that there was a hope in this future I cannot see.

It was like throwing a lit match in an abandoned
well,
you threw it into this void of darkness
just to see if there is anything left.

You're the only person who I trust enough
to show the cracks in my mentality
to you show my poorly crafted foundation.

My motivation for seeing you today
is that I want to be there to make your life just a
little more fun,
because I know every time you smile we are
closer to melting the sun.

Now it's not like I have a vendetta against the
sun, it's not like that.
it's just when I see something as mighty as the
star in our sky fail to match your glow,
I know that I won't need another light in my life.

Heartworm

It's hard to describe
but the ever wondering desire
that's been rooted in the back catalogue
of my heart has sprouted into
a life of its own.

There was no flash before the rumble
and the flames birthed by the remaining ember
from meeting you three years ago
under a shoddy build wall painted star gaze
surprised me.

I wonder what it feels like,
      To be unsuspecting,
and be labelled dangerous by
one who I only shared words with,
unknowing of the flint plating crafted around
them.

Perhaps it was expert craftsmanship,
but I was always decent at creating fire
out of words laced with secondhand desire.
and while you can't shape much out of it,
you can produce a flame.

Perhaps in a different life
would one be able to see the shadows
of two wisps playing in the dark,
and making fire out of the words
they shared amongst them.

The Nights We Remember

Whatever happened to the ambition
the youthful enthusiasm of dancing in the wild
as the synth rhythm guides each limb
in accordance to the sentiment given by the DJ?

We were nothing more than broke kids.

There was something beautiful about the way
our spirits
would float like wisps in the wind
freefalling past the worries that held us back
from seeing the 5am sun

The Lyrics to a Song I Never Heard but Always Wanted To

Where the hell have you been? You were hiding just inside the everyday normality of my story. When I first realised the waves you made on my shore I felt like I must learn how to play the piano just to replicate the pace my heart would get to every time I'm near you.

The comfort I get from being around you is like listening to music you never heard but adore the moment it comes on. You are like a song that everyone knows the words to. A modern-day Bohemian Rhapsody, a recapture of American Pie.

I struggle to grasp the concept of composure when the thought of you wakes me up in the morning. I drape my arm over my wishes of you being there. It's not just love, it's fantasy. Fantasy like the words lost in the winds between us, making me clutch the lyrics of a song that I want to sing for you.

I guess what I want to say is this, you are heard. I swear that the walls inch closer every time you speak just so they can listen to your voice more closely. The melody echoes off every surface, ever enchanting, promising me that if I stay silent I just might hear what beautiful sounds like.

Maybe I'll never learn how to play the piano, I know that the keys to happiness are strung across the seemingly growing distance between possibility and reality. Because the fact of the matter is, I don't know how to play any instruments. But I promise that I will always dance to the music I hope you'll play for me.

Could You Imagine

Could you imagine
the camera flash as time stops on frame
to forever hold the beauty of calmly existing
for that moment

Could you imagine
holding them dearly for their ever growing
warmth
gelling into a forever clearing reality, becoming
one
for that moment

Could you imagine
being there, seeing them again, present for you
smiling, never having left in the first place
for that moment

Could you imagine
floating in a dream now transparent with haze
covering your lips as the calm takes over
for that moment

Could you imagine
living in the future, presenting the now passed
memory,

at our garden, planting two thorned roses
with you again.

Mixed Messages

I never got to tell you that when I slept beside
you, I woke up just to hold
You always told me that I was lying when I said
your auburn eyes were
Beautiful describes the best parts of my dreams
in which I imagined kissing
You never believed me when I said that my love
was and would be forever
Undying be the whisper, describing the thoughts
of my adoration for
You never noticed how I would always make
sure the temperature was always
Perfect was the night when the forget-me-nots
convinced me to say that I love
You made me the happiest man in the world
when you said you loved me
Too

Chapters

We just got to the city,
and before we could claim a bed
we were celebrating manhood.

It took us years to get to here,
surviving childhood, the parties,
the fights, manhunts in the forest

We sat alone at a park bench,
the moon - our chaperone
laughing about everything we've done.

We were only boys then,
none of us had any clue
how short that chapter would be.

Minority

There is this pair of sweatpants,
they sit in the bottom left drawer of my dresser.
Sometimes
I like to picture myself wearing them.

That comfortable,
snuggly feeling.
Like a warm hug
from an old friend
you used to crush on.

It's such an out there concept,
- but imagine if it happened.
Me
wearing those sweatpants
from the bottom left drawer of my dresser.
Or that black hoodie
that my mom got me two Christmases ago
the one that she special purchased because so
it'd fit just right
Or any stained shirt ever
one that you can wear for comfort at home
because finally no one is watching.

I learned young

to button-up
so that there wouldn't be
as many eyes watching me today
so i can go and buy my favourite candy
from that gas station down the street.

And I always wondered
why some people's sunday best
was my only way to feel normal.

I was about 10
when I learned
that wearing comfortable
might get me stopped
by the police today.

I guess this is what it's like
to be true, north, strong, and free.

Bleeding Scars

They said to know my place.
You see it was a question I couldn't really face
because to question it would remind me of my
race.
Which for some reason is something people
want to erase.
It doesn't even make sense in the first place.

Whatever I did, it wasn't enough.
Every action treated as a plea to be forgiven,
like dad trying to get back with mom after
surprising her with an unexpected son
it was ridiculous. But I did it.
Whatever it took to try and convince them that I
was enough.

It took a lot of time.
A lot of time.

Eventually I grew to appreciate myself.
But like everyone who has done that, it doesn't
stop the bleeding.
Every word that has cut every major artery has
forever left a scar.

There is no reconstructive surgery for a broken
spirit.

It takes a long time to stop the bleeding.
It takes a long time to love yourself.

Crescent Gaze

Maybe it was the lighting,
but as you looked towards the rooms sky
I swore to you that the glistened dew stained
your cheekbones auburn.

It was the dimming glow that bothered mine.
I don't know if was the environment,
or the moon of currant, bleeding a signal that
made
the roaming mutts howl alongside you.

Your eyes, now faced with fears that knows
it can take over and plaster this town.
Fear subsiding into your crescent gaze
as you avoid looking towards anyone.

I know you won't hear me,
but I want to help you.

Insecure

It was very clear
the purring of the ceiling fan kept us awake
as the dew settled into your uncut backyard.
It grew colder.

Perhaps those men, fantastic
misconstrued across your dim ceiling
being blown about, reminding you
of those you wished for,
rather than the bastard.

To justify the means
is to understand the bastard as no more
than the tap which sap leaks from
for the one, insecure.

Someone To Be

I saw you there last night. To my surprise, you looked alright. Your smile gave me company and for that moment you silenced the past that haunted me.

I found comfort in the fact that I could tell you anything and everything. But In the back of my mind I couldn't help but see it. That the background was fading behind you and then I saw that you noticed too. For that moment I took the time to realise that we were running out of it, you were going to have to leave again.

While I panicked, trying to find something to say because I knew in the coming day you were going to be gone again. You looked at me as if to portray the words "It's going to be okay".

We both knew, We both knew that this may be the last time. As you faded away, you did find something to say. You said: "Move on Move on from this, You have somewhere to be. You got someone to be".

And then I awoke.

To Be Better

I wish I cared
about myself
the same way
I do others.

I live life tired
ike a asteroid
praying for that day
where I find home.

I hope to live
my life
a protagonist,
with a story to tell.

Until then,
I can only promise tomorrow,
hoping for one day
to be better.

Almost; or Bird Watchers

Our shoulders were almost touching,
while we walked side by side.
You're talking about your hometown.
Your gravity is pulling me in,
whispering's alright

We're touching now, yet not.
You held my shoulder
and shown me a bird you've been looking for
and how it reminded you
of bird watching with your mom.

We're no longer touching,
and I remember what it's like to fight for breath.
For the first time in a long time, I am fragile.
In a world that ignores sensitivity,
you believe me.

I almost said it.
All I want is one ounce of any strength I can
muster.
Enough to tell you every single thing I have ever
felt.
To find love in your cheekbones,
are you willing to let a stranger in?

I want you close because it's been cold lately,
and life is hard and my neck is aching.

Almost.

We Wait 'Til the Broken Hours

There are ambient roars of someone showering
upstairs,
and hums of laundry and emotional repairs.
It's been a long day now, and we all break
somehow.

Truth is you have no clue where to begin.
All those walls, they are caving in
It's beautiful in the broken hours.

In the broken hours, your lungs fill
and the night holds your eyes to your lids,
and your insides to your ins - you're wavering.

'Til the morning comes, everything is now
What isn't broke, will break somehow
Your giving in and letting go lets you in.

You rest your head into the ground
tensing until your calm comes around
there is a steep hill and a long way down.

After a blink of eternity there's a shy night sky.

Every morning a resurrection, shaking off all the dead
Le's have another go at it.

In Memory of You

I thought the stop sign was taller, I thought the trees were larger, I thought the grass was much greener when I walked here with my father. Now the grass is brown, the trees have been cut down, road signs lay on the ground The bond that we had Is nowhere to be found.

This is street I used to walk, it seemed longer when I was younger. Then I began to wonder what to categorise this feeling under. The rose-colored glasses have been taken off. Both of us knowing that if I see you you'll get a fist-full of fuck off.

I go back to the bar you used to frequent, to find myself not surprised you still do. You accidently looked in my direction, with a reaction that says: "Oh it's you." This is the place you hideaway with all the other busy men. I look at them all drowning themselves. I feel sorry for all their children.

I was one of them, asking my mother for my father. I was humbled when I found out about your other sons and daughters. With a smirk I

waltz up to the stool beside you, you tried to
look away, you didn't have a response for what I
came to say.

Hello, my dear father. looks like you've finally
been found. I don't want you to be bothered, but
how about you buy your forgotten son his first
round?

Putting the Dog to Sleep

You were my best friend.

The one who I could talk to, the one who battled strays and bandaged my wounds in the war that was childhood. We were partners in fighting through hounds and pounds of pressure that built up each day. I still remember hearing the story of how you were found, only days old and tied to a fence in a field long abandoned.

And despite the beginning of your story, you lived your life as my hero. My entire childhood is covered in your shed golden fur. You were the one who was there when my father left, the one who did everything in their power to convince me that I was safe until your last breath. So even to this day I consider it an unrivalled tragedy when I found you fighting with death.

You had cancer, and were old, and were scarred, and I was scared. It was time for you to go. I remember laying you in the back of our battered Montana, and tied around your neck our childhood bandana. I swear that you knew what was happening when we got there. The vet said it would be painless, I asked her after if it ever is.

In your final moments I discovered what beauty looked like. As I held out my hand, you put your paw in my palm. A trade secret that nobody knew because the world was convinced old dogs can't learn new tricks. But you were never an old dog. You were my best friend. So when I watched your life fade away, so did mine. I learnt then what it was like to be alone.

But like the strays you slayed for me, I battled death. We ran away and hid in the backyard. As I dug into the soil to play our last game of hide and seek, I found the beauty in death. In your final hiding spot, I planted a pine tree and grew a garden that you could trample through one last time.

I smile every time I think of you and how we defeated death together, our final victory. I find happiness when I remember that you're just hiding in my childhood, a living memory.

What Comes After

Dear Little Me,

I think about you often, and I remember the days when you wished to be well known and worldly. I might not have gotten there yet, but I will tell you that some days there are so many stars in the sky, you wouldn't believe it.

There aren't flying cars yet, but there are a few cool things. The adult stuff never stops being scary, but you'll find that you're not alone. You'll realise that everyone is a child in adult clothes, and you'll find peace in that.

You will meet so many people, and some of them may even love you, or at least like you a little bit. Just make sure in between conversations that you never lose your laugh, and to always help people find theirs.

You will have loved, and lost. Some people you will have already talked to for the last time, and you will wish there was more to say but everything has already been said. Nobody will

tell you how much that will hurt, but you will
always have people around you.

There will be nights where you are all alone, but
also days in which you will stand on the coast of
an ocean and wonder why you need anybody at
all. Then, you will remember who you are doing
this all for. Reach for those around you. Friends
can be family too.

I cannot tell you what comes after that, I'll write
to you when I do. Just remember to be hopeful
and have as much fun as possible. Don't be
afraid to fall in love as many times as it takes,
and try to smile just a little bit longer. You will
know the way.

Sincerely,
Older Little You

PS. You will learn to love yourself, ask for help
more, and always remember your story.